Bookkeeping

The Ultimate Guide to Bookkeeping for Small Business

(Working Less and Making More in the Bookkeeping Industry)

Robert Barratt

Published By **Jackson Denver**

Robert Barratt

Bookkeeping: The Ultimate Guide to Bookkeeping for Small Business (Working Less and Making More in the Bookkeeping Industry)

ISBN 978-1-998901-84-5

No part of this guidbook shall be reproduced in any form without permission in writing from the publisher except in the case of brief quotations embodied in critical articles or reviews.

Legal & Disclaimer

TABLE OF CONTENTS

CONTENTS

Chapter 1: What's New in Bookkeeping for Small Business?

Bookkeeping is always changing and new software is always coming out. Let's look at some of these techniques and software programs that are out there for you to use as a small business owner.

Open a Business Bank Account

You want to see your business succeed. However, how do you keep your personal finances separate from your business finances? The answer is simple; just open a business bank account.

It is extremely hard to see how your business is doing if you combine your business revenue and expenses with your personal. The best way is to check with your bank first to see if they have a business account available.

Using a spreadsheet is basic. Although, what if your business has inventory, employees, vendors, etc.? This is when an accounting or bookkeeping software could come in handy. My recommendation is QuickBooks or Xero as they both provide for these types of accounts.

Choose the Best Bookkeeping Software for your Business

Choosing a software can vary based on your needs. At minimum, you will need a ledger or cashbook. The cashbook that would include the general journal and the ledges can easily be done using a spreadsheet like Microsoft Excel or Google Sheets. Remember, Google Sheet will allow you to save it through Google and have access to the file anywhere you are.

QuickBooks and Xero may not be the best for your business. Sometimes, the most difficult part is finding the software that works the best for your needs.

Let's look at a few different bookkeeping applications that may get you started. I will include QuickBooks and Xero.

Intuit QuickBooks Online

QuickBooks Online is by far the best accounting and bookkeeping software for small businesses. I like that you can link it to your bank account. This makes it easy to use and track money when linked to your business account. It makes it easy to reconcile the business account and the books. Although there is so much more to QuickBooks Online.

Just a few of the features within QuickBooks Online include:

Invoicing

Expense Tracking

Inventory Management

Purchase Ordering

Reporting

As your business grows, you can upgrade your account between the top three tiers. This will allow you to have everything you need for your small business. Another part that is great about QuickBooks Online is that there are apps for your phone both through Android and iOS devices. The software is also compatible with most third-party applications.

QuickBooks Online also offers some of the best pricing. There are four tiers of pricing, depending on what you need for your business. It also offers a 30-

day free trial. However, if you want to just jump right into it and go for the paid versions you will get a 50% discount for the first six months. That means if you are just starting your business you will have six months to make a little extra profit and get established before you need to pay full price.

The most basic is the Self-Employed plan. This plan is $10 per month. It is designed for independent contractors and freelancers. It allows the following:

Track Mileage

Track Income and Expenses

Create Invoices

Accept Payments

Run Reports

Keep in mind the Self-Employed plan cannot be upgraded to a higher tier. It will require you to create and set up a new account.

The next tier is the Simple Start plan. With this plan, a single user is supported and costs $15 per month. This plan includes the following:

Track Mileage

Track Income and Expenses

Create Invoices

Accept Payments

Run Reports

Send Estimates

Track Sales and Sales Tax

The next tier is the Essentials plan. This plan supports multiple users and costs $35 per month. This plan includes:

Track Mileage

Track Income and Expenses

Create Invoices

Accept Payments

Run Reports

Send Estimates

Track Sales and Sales Tax

Bill Management

Time Tracking

The last tier is the Plus plan. This plan also allows for multiple users and costs $50 per month. This plan includes:

Track Mileage

Track Income and Expenses

Create Invoices

Accept Payments

Run Reports

Send Estimates

Track Sales and Sales Tax

Bill Management

Time Tracking

Track Inventory

Create Budgets

Pay Independent Contractors that use the 1099 form

Like most small business, you will eventually have employees that you will need to pay. With QuickBooks Online, you can add this feature to any of the top three tiers for an additional monthly cost.

The best part is QuickBooks Online is very user friendly and easy to use. This software also has a good timesaving feature that you need in any good accounting and bookkeeping program. It will keep track of due dates for invoices, sync your business bank account, track your credit card transactions, and so much more. This allows you to focus more time on the business and less time on the books while maintaining accurate bookkeeping throughout your business and giving you a great outlook of the financials of the business. Another good timesaving feature that puts QuickBooks Online on top is that you can send out invoices to customers, allowing them to pay online at a click of a button.

Like with any application, things tend to go wrong with the program itself. That is why QuickBooks Online offers both phone and chat support. You can access this from the company website making it easier and quicker to get issues resolved and have you up and running again without missing a sale.

QuickBooks Online is account approved. This means that no matter what your needs are you can give your accountant access to your books. Remember, that your account will not take up a spot in your users that you give access to.

Like all programs there are some limitations, although with QuickBooks Online it seems like the sky is the limit. The limitations really lay within the mobile apps. Here are the things you can do with the mobile apps:

Send Invoices

Reconcile Transactions

Take photos of receipts and attach to expenses

View customer information and add new customers

View dashboard data, such as account balance, profit and loss reports, and open and past due invoices.

After looking through what the app can do, if you feel like that works perfect then QuickBooks Online is the perfect software for you. However, if you prefer doing most of your accounting and bookkeeping through your phone, then there is another accounting and bookkeeping software choice for you.

Xero

If you would rather use a PC or a Mac, Xero has a lot to offer. Xero is by far the best accounting and bookkeeping software for Mac users. It easy to use and learn. What I like about Xero are the videos. Everything you do in Xero will have a video that will help you learn the software.

Xero also has comparable prices and is listed into three different plans. The starter plan is $9 per month. It does have some limitations. The features of the starter plan are:

Unlimited Users

Limit to Five Invoices per month

Limit to Five Bills per month

Limit to 20 Transaction Reconciliations per month

The standard plan is $30 per month. This includes:

Unlimited Users

Unlimited Invoices

Unlimited Bills

Unlimited Transaction Reconciliations

Payroll for up to Five Employees

The premium plan is $70 per month. Which includes:

Unlimited Users

Unlimited Invoices

Unlimited Bills

Unlimited Transaction Reconciliations

Payroll for up to 10 Employees. Note: this can be adjusted to support more employees if needed.

Supports Multiple Currencies. Note: this is a great feature if you do international business.

The best part is that there are not any long-term contracts for using Xero. That means you can change at any time without having additional fees. There is also a free 30-day trial to let you try and find out if it will be the best for your business.

Much like QuickBooks Online, Xero also has many timesaving features. You can send out invoices electronically, which also allows for your customers to pay online easily. You can also turn quotes and estimates into invoices with only a few clicks. This allows for you to give a customer a quote and if they agree to go with your services you can turn that quote into an invoice and get paid.

With your business bank account linked to Xero, the system will allow you to set scheduled payments and manually pay the bills. This helps save time and ensures that all bills are paid on time and you do not need to worry about past-dues and late fees.

If you need to claim an expense that occurred, then Xero will help you to record, manage, claim, and reimburse the expense claims. You can also add expenses easily and attach the receipt images.

Xero has some great inventory management tools available for small businesses that do not offer services and instead sell merchandises that are kept in inventory. Here you can track your inventory and show how much inventory you have in stock.

As I mentioned with QuickBooks Online, it has limitations when it comes to mobile apps. Xero is one of these programs that allows for great mobile accessibility. The mobile app for Xero allows you to:

Create and Send Invoices

Add Receipts

Attach Billable Expenses to Customer Invoices

Submit Expense Reports

Reconcile Transactions

Access your Dashboard for Realtime View of your Cash Flow

Use an additional app for Employees for Submitting Time Sheets, Request Time Off, and View Paystubs

One thing that sets Xero apart from other software is that it also has the capability to have a developer design and customize your own app by providing the API to allow for integration to your Xero account.

There is also a 24/7 customer support for those times that you have issues with your account, allowing you to have your books back up without losing the sale. However, there is one drawback to Xero. There are not many accountant and bookkeepers who know the software. Therefore, it brings in limitations to finding someone to keep your books.

Zoho Books

If you are a sole proprietor, freelancer or E-Commerce with a home-base business, then this is a great bookkeeping software for you. It is easy to use and affordable. It will allow you to connect with all your accounts and it covers all the basic needs of your business.

Zoho Books offer three pricing plans. The basic plan is $9 per month. This plan only supports one user and allows you to add 50 contacts. Other features include:

Reconcile Transactions

Create Invoices

Track Expenses

Manage Projects

Manage Time Sheets

The standard plan is $19 per month and supports 2 users. It also allows for 500 contacts to be added. This plan includes:

Reconcile Transactions

Create Invoices

Track Expenses

Manage Projects

Manage Time Sheets

Track Bills

Track Vendor Credits

Add Reporting Tags to your Transactions

The professional plan is $29 per month and allows for 10 users. This plan also allows for unlimited contacts. It also includes:

Reconcile Transactions

Create Invoices

Track Expenses

Manage Projects

Manage Time Sheets

Track Bills

Track Vendor Credits

Add Reporting Tags to your Transactions

Create Sales Orders

Create Purchase Orders

Manage Inventory

Zoho Books has one of the best customer services and support. The phones are open 24 hours a day, five days a week.

One disadvantage of Zoho Books is that it does not offer payroll services. If you have employees than you would need software that is for payroll. If you do not have employees then this is the best for you and your business.

FreshBooks

I mentioned earlier that there is software for bookkeeping that is great for those who want more accessibility through mobile apps. What makes FreshBooks the best is that you can find almost all the features in the mobile app that you have on the website. Keep in mind, if your business has inventory then this may not be the software for you.

Most all the software we have been talking about is based on features. With FreshBooks, the pricing is based on active clients. For the Lite plan, it is $15 per month and allows you to bill up to five clients. The plus plan is $25 per month and allows you to bill up 50 clients. The premium plan is $50 and allows to bill up to 500 clients.

For each of the plans you can add contractors at no additional cost. However, if you need to add employees it is an extra $10 per month for each employee. Contractors and employees can view different parts of the books.

Employees can:

View and Create Invoices and Expenses

View the Dashboard

Generate Reports

Contractors can:

View Projects they have been Assigned to

Track Time towards the Assigned Projects

Create and Send You Invoices for their Time

FreshBooks also has some timesaving features. You can create, send and manage invoices easily. This can be done from your computer or mobile app. It also allows for faster payments and makes tracking your expenses easy and allows for project management and time tracking.

With all software, customer service is a must. You will find both phone and email support. However, it is not 24/7 support. They do have hours between 8 a.m. to 8 p.m. eastern standard time Monday through Friday. With such great interface of mobile app then they also have support for those issues that may arise as well.

Wave Accounting

That brings us to the last bookkeeping software we are going to look at, Wave Accounting. Wave Accounting is great if you do not have much equity to start with, as this software is free. Yes, that's right, I did say free.

Wave Accounting is designed for very small businesses with 10 employees or fewer and no inventory. If your business offers services, then you may want to try it out. If you plan on growing your business, eventually you will need to transition to another form of software.

Keep in mind, what keeps Wave Accounting free is the use of advertising. That means it will not only post advertising on the software while you use it, but it will also include its branding on your communications with customers.

You can also add credit card processing for small fee per transaction. The same goes for payroll processing as this can be added for $15 per month as well as an additional $4 per employee per month.

Keep in mind, Wave Accounting does still offer the basics for the needs of your company. With the advertising, if you want to have your business separated from all the ads, then you may want chose a different software such as Zoho Books.

Create a Logo

One thing that will set your business apart from the rest is the business logo you create. This logo will be displayed on invoices, business cards, brochures, website, etc.

This should represent your business. You do not need to spend a lot of money on a good design. Search around and you will find a lot of sites that offer logo design for cheaper.

If you have some creative talent and want to create your own you can do that as well. A great place to start is through https://www.canva.com. This site is user friendly and free, although you do not need to use this site. You can easily create it in Word, Photoshop, Paint, etc. Make sure to save your logo as a JPG or PNG. If you use Word, then hit print screen and copy it into Paint so that you can save it in the proper format. Chose a good size for the logo and crop if needed. You may want to save different sizes as well. For example, you may have one size for your invoices, a size for your business cards, and a size for your letterhead when sending out emails and letters on behalf of the business.

Monthly Bookkeeping Reports

Many times, businesses start to struggle because they do not know how the business is doing from the beginning. A good rule of thumb is to actively have the books up-to-date and always accurate. This will help when you do reports.

Also, make sure you are pulling the reports monthly. Do not just wait until the end of the quarter or year. If you have the reports each month it will give you a better understanding of how your business is doing and can help you make changes, if needed, for the following month.

With that said, I also want you to understand it is also just as important to do quarterly and yearly reports. This will help you judge how the business is doing overall throughout the year and throughout the years.

Hire Employees

Adding employees to your business is not always the easiest to keep up with. It brings new responsibilities as you will need to keep track and pay their wages. One thing that can help with this is the bookkeeping software applications that we have discussed. It is worth ensuring you have the payroll feature if you have employees. Your employees rely on this paycheck.

Granted with payroll, you also have payroll taxes. This money belongs to the government. One thing that could help with this is to have a separate savings account within your business account for holding all the payroll taxes. That way when it comes time to pay the government the money is already set aside.

Make sure you are filing the correct documents for payroll on time otherwise you could encounter added fines.

Try New Systems

There are so many systems out there that will help your business succeed. We have talked about a few of the software programs used for bookkeeping. However, if you add too many systems at once it could be overwhelming for you, your employees, and your customers.

As the business owner, you need to carefully select the applications you need for your business. A good rule of thumb is only try the systems that are needed for either maintenance or growth. If your business does not need it for either one of these, then do not add them! One thing that could help with this is having a website or mobile app designed that integrates everything you need for your business. You can add a feature that allows you, your employees, and your customers to access the same app, but based on their credentials they will only have access to what is needed for them.

Keep in mind, if you introduce one system at a time you will be able to give everyone a chance to learn the system before introducing the next.

Chapter 2: The Balance Sheet

A balance sheet is going to show the assets of the company, the liabilities of the company, and the net worth, or the owner's equity. The balance sheet will work along with the other financial documents that we have talked about in order to show a complete picture of the financial state of that company. If you hold onto stocks of that company, it is a good idea to understand more about the balance sheet, such as how it is structured, the best ways to look over and understand the sheet, and even tips for reading through the balance sheet.

How Can I Use this Financial Document?

The balance sheet is going to be split up into two parts. These two parts are going to be based on an equation, and they must either end up equaling each other or coming out so that they are balanced, or something is wrong with your numbers. The formula that is needed to work with the balance sheet will include this:

Assets = Liabilities + Shareholder's Equity

What all this means is that all the assets, or the money used to operate the company, need to be balanced out by the financial obligations of the company, along with any of the equity investment that comes back to that company, and then they will be known as that company's retained earnings.

The assets are important because they are what the company will use in order to operate the business. The equity and the liabilities are going to be what will support those assets. The owner's equity, which can be known as the shareholder's equity, if the company is publicly traded, will include any of the money that the shareholders invested in that company. It can also include any retained earnings as well. This is important because it is going to represent the funding sources for that particular business.

One way that the balance sheet is different than the income statement we talked about before is that the balance sheet we talked about earlier is more of a snapshot that showcases the financial position of that company right then and there. If the accountant does this financial document on May 21, 2018, then the balance sheet will show where the company is on that date. It won't cover February 21 to May 21. It just shows May 21.

The Balance Sheet for the Securities and Exchange Commission

Just like the bank wants you to put together a balance sheet to take a look at whether they think you can do well with any credit they offer, the government is going to require that any company that is traded publicly will put together a balance sheet, usually each quarter, to show to their shareholders.

This balance sheet can be important because it will allow all potential and current investors to see a good snapshot of the finances of that company. In addition to some other things, the balance sheet is going to show you all the value of the stuff that the company owns, right down to the office supplies that the employees use, the amount of debt that the company is taking care of right now, and how much inventory is in the warehouse. It can even tell the investors about how much money the business will have available to work with through the short-term.

This balance statement is going to be one of the first financial statements that you should analyze when you want to see the value of the company. Before you can learn how to analyze this balance sheet, it is important to know how it is structured.

Before we get into this too much though, you need to understand that the limited partnership, limited liability company, and the corporation balance sheets are going to be a lot different from the regular household balance sheet. This is mainly because these companies have a lot of complex items in their accounting records to keep the company going. This is why many of these companies rely on an accountant to help them get it done.

Businesses are often faced with many difficult questions that others may not know the answers to, such as how to depreciate out the costs for some of their business expenses, how to record the lease obligations, how to account for the expenses of construction at the power plan, and so much more.

No matter how overwhelming it can seem in the beginning to figure out all the different parts of the balance sheet, it is actually pretty simple once you have looked at a few. The best way to get through the balance sheet is to remember that the purpose of this financial statement is to answer three basic questions for anyone who is looking at that sheet. These three main questions that the balance sheet should answer include:

What does the company have? These will be the assets of the company.

What does the company owe on? These will be the liabilities of the company.

What is left over for the owners of that business if they were to pay off all their debts? This one is going to be the shareholder equity or the book value.

These are pretty advanced terms and fancy words, but they are there to help give the investor a good idea of where the business is at that time. If you can remember the objective of the balance sheet, all those fancy words and accounting complexities won't seem as overwhelming when you take a look over it later.

One thing to remember is that unlike some of the other financial statements, the balance sheet is not going to cover a range of dates. The information that is present in the balance sheet is going to be good as of the date that is on the balance sheet, but it won't be able to tell you any date ranges in the process. If you are looking to deal with this issue when calculating many of the accounting ratios, then the best way to do this is to work with the averagely weighted figures of the balance sheet.

An example of this is if you would like to figure out what the average value of inventory was for that year for the company. You would be able to do this by taking the value of the inventory at the previous yearend, add it to the inventory's value at the end of this year, and then divide them by two.

This is a fast trick that will help you to avoid any distortions by ending period figures that may or may not be able to reflect what occurred throughout that year accurately. For example, if the manufacturing business was able to pay off all the debt it had in the year, and this showed that there was $0 in liabilities on this balance sheet, but then there was a line there to show the interest expense on your income statement, this could be confusing.

By taking the time to weigh the average debt outstanding from the balance sheet over that same period, you may be able to get a better idea of what the business has going on here and why they listed some interest costs on the income statement but not on the balance sheet.

What Are the Different Types of Assets?

Next, we need to take a look at some of the assets that the company needs to keep track of. Remember that these assets are going to help the company do its normal operations. There are two types of assets that each business will need to pay attention to, including current assets and noncurrent assets.

Current Assets

Current assets are going to be any that the company owns that have a lifespan that is a year or less. This means that the asset has to be easily changed over to cash if the company needs to. Such assets will include inventory, accounts receivable, and cash or cash equivalents.

Cash, which is the most fundamental and most commonly thought about the current asset, can also include checks and bank accounts that are not restricted. Cash equivalents are going to be assets that are very safe, but which can also be turned into cash quickly if the company needs. The US Treasury is a good example of this. And then there are the accounts receivables, which are going to show the reader any of the obligations that customers and others owe to the company over the short-term. These sometimes happen if a company allows the customer to use credit to purchase the product or service.

Inventory is an important current asset as well. Inventory can include things like the raw materials to make a product, the products that are still in the process of being created, and the finished goods. Each company is going to be different, and the exact way that the inventory account looks is going to be different. For a manufacturing firm, there may be a lot of raw materials, but a retained firm wouldn't have any raw materials.

Noncurrent Assets

These noncurrent assets are going to be any that you are not able to turn into cash very easily, which the company doesn't plan to turn into cash soon. These also include items that will last more than a year. Tangible assets such as land and buildings are included in this. Sometimes, the intangible items will be added to this as well.

What Are the Different Liabilities?

Another part of the balance sheet is the liabilities. These are going to be any financial obligations that the company owes to an outside party. Similar to the assets above, these will fall under the idea of being either a current liability or one that will last long-term.

The long-term liabilities are going to be any of the debts that the company has that will be due in more than a year from that balance sheet date. The current liabilities though are going to be any liabilities that need to be paid off within a year. This could include some of the shorter-term borrowings or even the latest interest that you paid on a longer loan.

The company needs to properly list out all the liabilities that they have on this balance sheet. This helps the investor or the lender know how many debts and obligations that the company is dealing with, and then they can compare this to the profits of the company to see where the company stands financially. This information is much more important to making sound decisions for the investor or the lender compared to just looking at the profits.

For example, a company may have some great profits, but if they have such high debts that they can barely keep up with them, then those high profits don't mean anything. The investors and lenders want to make sure that the company is able to handle their debts and pay them off, while still making a profit and paying their investors before they put any money into it.

Shareholders' Equity

The shareholder's equity is going to be the beginning amount of money that the owners and others put into the business. If at the end of that year, the company wants to take their net earnings and reinvest it back into the company, then these earnings need to move over to your income statement and then placed into the equity account for the shareholder to make it work. This account is important because it will represent the net worth of the company.

The balance sheet is so important to a business. It gives a great snapshot of the finances of a business and can give analysts, investors, and lenders a good idea of where the business stands financially. Filling it out properly is going to make a big difference in how people view your company.

CHAPTER 3: Financial Statements

What is a Financial Statement?

A financial statement is a report prepared by a company that shows the performance of the company and status at a particular time with data obtained from the company. A suitable financial statement is made up of the balance sheet, income statement and equity statement.

The financial statement is one of the most important reports of the company that investors, shareholders, the public, as well as government agencies look forward to obtaining. The statement is very important for the company to analyze its position, health and its future and with the financial statement, the company can project its future and plan for an increase in profit.

You cannot go to an investor and ask them to be part of your business without a financial statement so that they can analyze your business. With the statement, the investor will study the equity, assets, liabilities and other accounting elements to check if their investment will be worthwhile.

The financial statement is also essential for the company to know how they stand and what decisions to take in order to improve their business. With the statement, a company can get to know what risks there are in their investments and they can make a decision on the level of risk to take in future investments.

Why Do We Need Financial Statement?

The financial statement of a business serves different purposes to a different set of people and the statement is provided for dissemination. There are parts of the financial statement that may be of interest to certain parties as they will divulge that information that helps decision making, checking the status of the company and planning.

In essence, the financial statement provides accounting information about the company, which shows how the business is being run, the way cash and assets are used and what is left after a certain period of time.

The production of financial statements is a collation of bookkeeping for a set period of time. It is expected that a company provides its financial statement to shareholders and the public, so the information provided for that period will be collated and presented. That is why it is important to record every piece of financial information and transactions in an ordered account method for ease in using them to produce such information.

The financial statement is made up of different parts, which provide a different interpretation of how the operation is carried out, the cash flow and how the assets of the company are used.

The income statement is an important financial statement of the company and one that investors are primarily interested in analyzing. From the income statement, the profitability of the Company can be ascertained, as it shows the volume of sale and how the company spends money - that is its expenses. A good income statement shows that the company is healthy and can generate income for investors who will be assured of profit in due time.

The income statement mentioned contains all the expenses the company has operated on over time. With these statements, the person studying the statement can find out the trends within the company. With such knowledge, a decision can be made that will affect the business based on the knowledge of how the company has been spending its cash in their expenses statement.

The balance sheet is another important financial statement that will show the present state of the company at the period the statement was presented. This statement will enable you to analyze the future of the company and if the present way of running the business is sustainable. With this point of view, you can make a decision on how the operation of the business will be handled. From the statement, the liquidity of the business, its funding and debt status of the company can be analyzed. Major decisions affecting businesses can be made when such information is studied.

The statement of cash flow shows the cash movement and the purposes of the operations made. A business owner will want to know the flow of cash and the purposes that cash was used for and how this affects the business. Such statements will determine specific spending in the next business budget. Such statements are important to planning the next business period, after the statement had been produced.

The financial statement contains all major information analyzed, which is a compilation of data recorded over a period of time. All these statements are important for the shareholders, public, investors and for the people running the business.

The aggregates of financial statements are used for:

This can be used by investors to analyze the prices of the business if they intend or are interested in investing in the business. The information is required by the investors as they want to know how the business has been faring over time and determine the profitability of their investments.

Government entities also require the financial statements of a business to estimate the tax or exemption offered to the business. You can calculate your tax returns, which will enable you check for errors by government entities that come to analyze your accounts.

With proper financial statements, you will also be able to check for bank errors, which will save you from paying more than you should pay.

Financial statements are required by lenders to determine if your business is qualified for credit facilities. They will analyze your information to ascertain that the information provided is accurate, which will determine the status of the company to receive credit.

Financial statements provide the public with information on how the business is being operated for a public company.

The financial statement is also essential for internal decision making of the company. The statement, which provides information on how the company is being run, will be used to make future decisions that will affect the business.

The financial statements are a compilation of various information and are used for different purposes depending on who is viewing it.

Understanding the Balance Sheet, Income Sheet and Statement of Cash Flow

In grasping the important of the financial statement and learning how to prepare financial statements, we have to understand the various statements that sum up the financial statement. In this category, we have the balance sheet, income sheets and statement of cash flow.

We have mentioned the importance and usefulness of these financial statements, but now we need to grasp a full understanding of each statement, learn how to prepare them and how helpful they are individually. We are going to look at these statements one at a time.

Understanding Balance Sheets

The balance sheet is a summing up of the company's assets, liabilities and the shareholders equity, a report that is produce at the end of a fiscal year. This statement has a date at the top of it to show when it was reported, which will be helpful in planning for the next fiscal year.

The balance sheet takes into account all the information on assets and equity for the business year before the final report.

The formula for the balance sheet is:

Assets = Liabilities + owner's equity

With the above formula, you can easily calculate the balance sheet, but the difficulty remains in knowing what sort of information to use in calculating the balance sheet.

In accounting, one of the main challenges faced by the bookkeeping staff is to know the particular elements to input and where to input these elements. In the case of the balance sheet, what are the assets, liabilities and owner's equity?

You can identify and calculate the elements in the balance sheet:

You should look for and identify all the assets in the balance sheet for the particular period you intend to balance your account. This should be the present fiscal year of the company and ensure you do not include assets from the previous fiscal period. After you have located all the assets in that specific period, you then calculate the total assets of the company.

The next step is to search for all the liabilities in the fiscal period and calculate the total liabilities in a different list in the balance sheet. You cannot mix the assets and the liabilities in the balance sheets to get an accurate accounting of the balance sheet.

The next step is to calculate the total shareholders' equity on the balance sheet. Gather this information up from the records, calculate the total of the shareholders equity and sum it up with the liabilities already recorded on the balance sheet.

At this point, we have to calculate the total assets, which are a summing up of the total liabilities and total equity.

The above step is required to calculate the balance sheet and will require you to take every step meticulously so you pick out every element and come up with an accurate calculation. I would advise you to understand how to determine the assets, liabilities and equity of the company so that you know which of the elements to use to calculate and ensure you have an accurate calculation.

You can check the above topics where we discussed about assets, liability and equity to get an understanding as to how to identify the elements of the balance sheets.

With the balance sheet, you can easily identify how funding of the business is carried out. The assets of the business can be funded with liabilities, such as debts or stockholders earnings. This is some of the information you can get at a glance from a balance sheet. You can determine the capital and if it is from a loan or stockholders' earnings or recapitalization from the owners of the company. The business can also be funded by debts, which can be loans obtained and this will be stated on the balance sheets in the calculations made on the assets of the business.

While the assets of the company will be listed in the liquidity order, the liabilities listed on the balance sheet will be listed in the order they are to be remitted.

What to Include on the Balance Sheet

The balance sheet will be comprised of the following:

Assets

The asset on the balance sheet will contain the following:

List of liquid assets will include cash and any cash equivalents. The cash equivalent will also include treasury bills and other financial deposit, which may stand as an equivalent for cash.

You can also list money owed to the company by clients for services rendered or products acquired. These are part of the assets since transactions have already been completed.

You should also list inventories that are properties owned by the business.

Liabilities

The liabilities that are included in the balance sheet are also made up of the following:

All the debts of the company including short terms loans and long term loans.

Tax paid, rent paid and other utility payments.

Wages paid to workers should be included.

Dividends paid to shareholders is also another form of a liability.

Shareholders

The shareholders' equity in the balance sheet should include:

The shareholders equity is money that the company owes to the shareholders after all the company debts have been paid off. The shareholders also have a share of the assets of the company if the assets are completely sold off. This can easily be summed up as the company's total assets with its total liabilities subtracted.

You should also take into account the returned earnings that were not paid to shareholders as dividends, which will be regarded as retained earnings.

Income Statements

The Income statement is a combination of the revenue, earnings, expenses, net income and earnings per share over a range of time. The range of time is one of the features of the income statement that makes it different from the balance sheet. The income statement is produced over a specific range of time, from annual statements to quarterly statements.

One other aspect that makes the income statement differ from the balance sheet is that you need data from other yearly income statements over the years for comparison. The income statement is essential in calculating the expenses of the company and is used in making any financial decision involved in the business. With the income statement, you can determine if your business is running at a deficit or are you on the positive side. With this determination, you can consider where to make changes so as to ensure that you do not run at a loss.

The income statement is important to investors and other outsiders who require the statement of the company. But it is very important for the business owners as a means to analyze how to keep the business heading in the right direction, which is to stay positive and make a profit.

Naturally, when your expenses are more than your revenue, you are in trouble with your business as you are spending more than you can earn.

The formula for income statement calculation is as follows:

Net Income = revenue – expenses

The steps below will guide you on how you can calculate your net income for your income statement.

You should make records of all the sales and earnings of the business in that particular time and make a total of all the revenues.

Make a list of all the expenses including the cost of running the business, totally all the expenses of the business for that particular period.

To get your net income, you should then subtract the expenses from your revenue to get your net income.

Now you must understand the importance of the income statement in determining the state of your business or how healthy the business is based on the income statement. A business with negative net income shows that the business is unhealthy, while a business with a positive net income is in a good state and will be much more likely to attract investors.

Understanding the Income Statement

The income statement is very important to investors, as well as the business owners, and usually requires a professional accountant to prepare the statement accurately.

To understand how to prepare an income statement, we have to look at the data required to produce the income statement.

Revenue

Revenue is money that comes into the company from either the services rendered, products sold or other forms of earning that come into the company. There are two main types of revenue, which include operating revenue and non-operating revenue.

Operating revenues are those that are earned from the direct business operations of the company including the services rendered by the company or product from the goods produced by the company. For example, in a soap production company, the operating revenue is the actual soap being sold.

Non-operating revenue includes earnings from non-operating services that do not include the sales of products from the company or the payment of services rendered by the company. The earnings or revenue in this case are not directly from the business. Non-operating services include:

The interest on cash in the bank.

Income received from rental of the company's assets.

Royalty payments.

Profit made from the sale of assets.

The non-operating revenues also include any other business that does not come from the direct sales of products or services produce by the business. These are the revenues you have to take into account to get the actual revenue in order to work out your future income and get the correct records of the business.

Expenses

Expenses can be referred to as the money spent in the operation of the business and we need the expenses carried over a certain length of time to calculate the income statement.

In gathering up the details of the expenses, we have to know what exactly we are looking for and what can be classified as expenses of the company. There are two kinds of expenses when it comes to accounting: we have primary expenses and secondary expenses.

Primary expenses are those that are directly involved in the running of the business, such as the payment of wages, procurement of goods in running the business, administration expenses, electricity bills, utility charges, sales commissions and other direct spending of the company.

The secondary expenses are those that are not directly linked to the operation of the business, such as losses in the sale of assets, interest paid, loans and debts and so on.

In order to get the actual expenses, we have to calculate the primary expense and the total expenses. The investors are interested in knowing how the business is managed in terms of the expenses, which can produce a red flag for them if the business is running in the negative. With this income statement the business owner will have knowledge on where to curb expenses for the business.

The Cash Flow Statement

The cash flow statement compliments the balance sheet and the income statement and shows how well a business can be funded to offset its debts. It also shows how the business will be able to cater for the expenses, such as operational cost, fund investment, as well as meet up to its general obligations.

Understanding Cash Flow Statement

The cash flow statement is different from the balance sheet and income statement because there is no formula for measuring cash flow. Rather, it shows you the information on how the cash flows into the system. This is a very important statement for investors to digest in order to understand the funding of the business and determine the strong capital base of the business.

Funding in business is important, especially the base funding, which we can refer to as "on the ground" running of the business. When there is a huge drawdown on basic funding of the business, it shows a huge risk for investors to invest in such a business. Because the investors will prefer not to invest in ventures that will start yielding profit in the future, but rather into sustaining sectors of the business.

There are three important sections that record the cash flow of a business, even as we have no formula for calculations of the cash flow statement. We are going to discuss these important sections in the statement below.

Operating Activities

The operating activities of the cash flow statement include any activities that involve cash coming in and going out in the operation of the business. The operational activities include cash in both accounts payable, accounts receivable, inventory, wages, income, cash receipts from the direct sales of goods and services, rents and anything involved in the direct operation of the business. The operational cash flow includes all records of cash flow involves in the operation of the business and this will require a professional accountant in running the business.

Investing Activities

These are activities of funding and cash flow that involve investing in the long term future of the company. The investing activity includes cash received from investors, the purchase and sales of assets and funds derived from investors during a merger and acquisition, sales and procurement of equipment, fixed assets and any long term investments in the company would be calculated in this category.

This section is a strong base for funding of the company, where investors are made to see that all of the operations of the company are running smoothly.

Chapter 4: Accounting Systems:

Principles

The first eight chapters of this book have explored the fundamentals of bookkeeping. These chapters have discussed the two types of bookkeeping systems – single-entry and double-entry; the two types of accounting methods – cash and accrual; the accounting and bookkeeping cycle from collecting records of business transactions, to recording transactions in a journal, to posting them in a ledger, to creating financial statements at the end of the accounting and bookkeeping cycle. Clearly, every business may face a multitude of varying challenges on any given day, so it is not possible to foresee every possibility you may encounter in your efforts in professional bookkeeping. However, the previous chapters have mentioned one concern that deserves additional attention.

The main function of bookkeeping is to allow business owners to formulate an accurate assessment of their business's overall financial condition and performance. This chapter explores some of the ways well-designed financial statements can help business owners, investors, and financial regulators accurately assess the current state of financial health of any given business, as well as its potential for increased profitability and growth.

Figure 10: Free Image

Knowing How to Run Your Business

Running a business effectively requires a broad range of knowledge and access to resources. Perhaps most important, the business owner must understand the value of the goods and services his or her business will be providing, and how to produce and deliver high-quality products and services. Consider the vast array of products and services that are available in both local and global markets:

- Consumer retail businesses such as department stores

- Hotels and restaurants

- Automobile dealerships and repair services

- Grocery stores

- Hobbies and other specialized interests, such as camping and outdoor living; musical instrument sales and instruction; pet supply stores, etc.

- Real estate and investing firms

- Legal and other professional service firms

- Advertising, sales, and marketing

- Technology supplies and service

The list is virtually endless. Each sector of business requires extensive knowledge not only of the specifics of the types of goods and services a given area of business should be able to provide, but also more general business knowledge, including advertising; personnel management; lead generation; occupational safety and health; public relations; and much more.

But regardless of the specific nature and the day-to-day details of operating your business, all businesses share one common aspect: bookkeeping is an essential daily function. It is true that providing quality goods and services that answer a genuine need or desire will always be one of the key aspects of success in the professional world. However, even a business that offers the highest quality goods and services can suffer and fail financially if they do not employ effective financial management tools.

Gaining Knowledge of a Business Through Bookkeeping

The three main types of financial statements – the balance sheet; the income statement; and the cash flow statement – each provide unique opportunities for gaining knowledge about any given business's core functions, profitability, competitiveness, and potential of further growth. Furthermore, the reason these three types of reports have been identified as the standard for financial statements that comply with Generally Accept Accounting Principles (GAAP) is because each type of report allows for the assessment of a different aspect of the business's performance. Together, all three allow for complete knowledge of the business's operations.

Many people may be interested in analyzing financial performance records to gain knowledge of a business. For example, the following occupational groups routinely seek to know businesses through a deep understanding of their business operations:

● **Creditors**. Any financial services organization that issues business loans will ask questions to determine whether the company has the capacity to repay. Often, they will request cash flow statements, so they can determine whether a company exercises appropriate discipline in the regulation of its expenses and income.

● **Investors**. If you work for or own a company that issues shares or is managed by investment partners, these individuals will be interested in examining financial statements for evidence that the company will be able to continue paying dividends to existing investors, or whether the company may be an attractive opportunity for future investors.

- **Management**. The goal of business management is to ensure that the company maintains operational efficiency and profitability. While ensuring that the needs of personnel and facilities are addressed is a very important aspect of management, no management team can assess whether their efforts are successful without examining the financial statements at the end of each accounting cycle.

- **Financial regulators**. Publicly held companies are required to submit financial statements to the Securities and Exchange Commission (SEC) to ensure GAAP compliance. In addition, any business may be audited by the IRS, and financial statements will be the main source of information.

Those interested in gaining knowledge of any business may choose to focus on one type of report over another depending upon their concerns. Specifically, each of the three types of reports may offer the following types of insights:

• **Balance sheets**: These reports can help investors and regulators determine such factors as asset turnover, receivables turnover, debt-to-asset ratios, and debt-to-equity ratios. Thus, the balance sheet provides a means to gain knowledge of a company's essential value at a given point in time.

• **Income statements**: These reports help investors and regulators determine a given company's gross profit margin, net profit margin, ratio of tax efficiency, and interest coverage.

78

- **Cash flow statements**: These reports help investors and regulators assess a company's ability to generate cash-driven revenue by showing the relationship between cash and overall earnings before interest, taxes, depreciation, and amortization. Thus, simply because a company can report a net profit at the end of the year does not necessarily mean that they have been successful in selling goods and services – this report can help determine whether profitability resulted instead from non-operating activity, such as loans or investments.

Analyzing Financial Reports

This section examines the specific types of financial analysis, as well as an overview of processes commonly employed to gain knowledge of businesses by examining their financial records.

Essentially, there are two types of financial analysis:

- Horizontal and vertical analysis
- Ratio analysis

Horizontal and Vertical Analysis

This type of financial analysis is typically used to analyze the results of income statements.

First, horizontal analysis compares the performance of certain aspect of a business's financial performance over two or more accounting periods. A horizontal analysis of any business may compare the change from one year to the next of a single aspect of its balance sheet – for example, a company's gross profits from sales. This analysis of the year-over-year (YoY) change in any given line item of a financial statement uses a specific formula:

Percentage of Change= (Value of Period N)/(Value of Period N-1)-1.

For example, let's calculate the YoY change in gross profits between 2017 and 2016 for Company ABC:

- In 2017, the company generated $4,000 gross profit in sales.

- In 2016, gross profit from sales was $3,000.

- YoY change is calculated as follows:

  o Percentage of YoY change = ($4,000 / $3,000) – 1

  o Percentage of YoY change = 1.33 – 1

  o Percentage of YoY change = .33

  o YoY change = 33%

Next, vertical analysis compares the line items of any given financial report within one single year to understand the significance of the relationships among the various statistics for that reporting year. For this example, we will consider the income statement for Company ABC. In the following illustration, you can see on the left the breakdown of the company's income; on the right, you can see an analysis of those numbers that shows the percentage of each figure in relation to revenue:

	2018
Revenue	500,000
COGS	(300,200)
Gross Profit	**100,800**
Depreciation	(500,000)

SG&A	(300,000)
Interest	(5,000)
Earnings before tax	**95,000**
Tax	(22,500)
Net earnings	**72,500**

Because this type of analysis compares statistical reporting data within one vertical column of figures, it is referred to as vertical analysis.

Ratio Analysis

Ratio analysis takes a different approach. Ratio analysis calculates the relative size or value of one statistic to another. This ratio is then used as a standard of comparison to determine how a company is performing – either in relation to a prior time period or to an industry standard. Generally, ration analysis should confirm expectations, but it can also indicate areas of concerns. There are several main categories of ratio analysis:

• Liquidity ratios measure the ability of a business to remain in operation by examining the following factors:

o Cash coverage ratios comparing available cash to pay interest;

o Current ratios measuring amount of liquid assets available to pay liabilities;

o Quick ratios, which are the same as current ratios, except that they exclude inventory;

o Liquidity index, which measures how long it will take to convert assets to cash.

- Activity ratios show how well a company is managing the use of its resources and include:

  o Accounts payable turnover ratios

  o Accounts receivable turnover ratios

  o Fixed asset turnover ratio

  o Inventory turnover ratio

  o Sales to working capital ratio

  o Working capital turnover ratio

- Leverage ratios measure the degree to which a company is relying on debt to maintain operations and includes the following:

  o Debt-to-equity ratio

  o Debt service coverage ratio

  o Fixed charge coverage ratio

- Profitability ratios measure the ability of a company to generate profit and include:

o   Break-even point ratio

o   Contribution margin ratio

o   Gross profit ratio

o   Margin of safety

o   Net profit ratio

o   Return on equity ratio

o   Return on net assets ratio

o   Return on operating assets ratio

Decision Making Through Effective Bookkeeping

Thus, there are two sides to effectively managing any type of business. Producing quality goods and services, selling them at competitive rates and prices, and ensuring that people are aware of your business are absolute essentials. Without these skills, no one would have any business to manage. It may be tempting to assume that you can make effective business decisions based exclusively on your expertise in your given field of professional work or your skill as a personnel manager. However, to make your business stand out and reach its full potential, you must harness the power of effective bookkeeping to gain insights into the ways your business operations can remain competitive.

The following six steps of the financial analysis process explain how a thorough understanding of the bookkeeping and accounting cycle can help you be a better business owner, or help you be a better bookkeeper for the business owners you serve:

Analyze the economics of the industry in which you are working.

Although GAAP-compliant bookkeeping and accounting methods apply across all industry lines, each industry will have its own particular characteristics. What types of goods or services does your industry produce? What is the industry standard method of producing and distributing these goods and services? Identifying the costs involved in these methods is known as a "value chain analysis," and you will be at a competitive disadvantage until you have a thorough understanding of your industry.

Establish a competitive strategy.

Consider the type of product or service your company offers. Is your product or service unique? What are your profit margins and access to other forms of capital? What about brand recognition? Have you assessed the demographic in which you will be offering goods and services? What strategy can you implement that will address all of these concerns?

Examine the financial statements.

Now that you have identified a specific business objective and a plan for achieving that objective, you can approach an analysis of the company's financial statements form an educated perspective. For each of the three types of reports, consider the following:

- Balance sheet: Does the company have sufficient assets to continue operating?

- Income statement: How successful is the company at generating revenue from sales of goods and services?

- Cash flow statement: Does the company exercise good judgment in managing its funds?

Conduct a thorough financial analysis.

Using the techniques of horizontal, vertical, and ratio analysis discussed earlier in this chapter, conduct a complete analysis of the company's performance. Focus specifically on areas you may have identified in the previous steps as needing improvement. How profitable is the company? Has performance been improving or declining? What does a financial analysis tell you about the areas that require greater attention?

Make recommendations

As the company's bookkeeper, you are in a unique position to contribute to a discussion of the direction of the company's direction for future growth and investment. Although market research and an assessment of the quality of the goods and services your company provides is a necessary part of this conversation, the hard date derived from a disciplined analysis of well-maintained and reliable accounting and bookkeeping records can provide invaluable insight.

Issue an official valuation of the company.

Especially if you are part of a publicly traded company, an annual statement that places a total value on the company can be the most important driver of success. If you are required to submit reports to the SEC, it is imperative that you show documentation of the reliability of your calculations. If you are a smaller, privately held company, a disciplined valuation can still allow you to benefit by appearing to be a more attractive investment to lenders, clients, and customers.

Chapter 5: Journals and Ledgers

In accounting or bookkeeping, every financial transaction is recorded into a journal (either digitally or manually) in order by date. A journal was more prominent during earlier periods, and it was traditionally called the book of original entry. This name came into prominence because accountants would record every financial transaction into a journal before posting them under their respective accounts into subsidiary ledgers or a separate general ledger.

The journals of business are maintained by using the rules of debit and credit that have been discussed under the single-entry system in the previous chapter.

Seven Types of Journals

There are different types of journals that are used to maintain and manage the financial records of different types of accounts and record different types of financial transactions. Some of these journal entries are only used under the double-entry system, whereas some of them follow the single-entry system of data collection. As discussed earlier, every financial transaction is first recorded into a journal before it is posted into subsidiary ledgers. It becomes rather difficult and complicated to obtain complete information for any financial transaction or assess the effects of these transactions on your business if all of them have been recorded in one common journal. It also becomes a rather time-consuming and arduous process to record every financial transaction into one journal. It is for this specific reason why we have now shifted to using different journals or ledgers instead of using one common journal. This becomes especially important for medium and large-scale businesses that are involved in many financial transactions on an everyday basis. This is called the classification of journals where you will maintain specific journals for specific types of transactions. These journals are also known as daily journals, special journals, or subsidiary journals. Large-scale businesses often record their transactions in these special journals along with a general journal. The primary types of journals in accounting are:

1. Purchase journals.

2. Sales journals.

3. Cash receipt journals.

4. Cash payment/disbursement journals.

5. Sales return journals.

6. Purchase return journals.

7. Proper journal/General journal.

It is very important to keep in mind that there are very few numbers of large businesses in any economy. Most economies or markets are dominated by medium-scale and small-scale industries, and these businesses always maintain a cashbook that is used to record cash receipts and daily cash payments. These businesses do not maintain a separate cash journal for recording these types of entries.

Purchase Journals

A purchase journal is a type of journal that is used to record the purchase of merchandise on credit for the purpose of selling them. However, any assets that are purchased on the account cannot be recorded in purchase journals. Most bookkeepers or accountants believe that these types of financial transactions should only be recorded in a multi-column purchase journal. For instance, the firm Pyle & Larson always tend to show their purchase of assets or supplies that are made on credit under a separate column or section in the purchase journals. Bookkeepers always credit payables of the account, and they also debit the office or asset supplies. However, it is better to avoid doing this; you should not record the transactions that involve the purchase of any other things that are made on credit into the purchase journal. It is always better to record these transaction entries into the general journal.

A single-column purchase journal is always used for recording the credit purchase of any type of merchandise. A single-column purchase journal will follow the same format in both periodic systems as well as perpetual columns. In periodic systems, the purchase accounts and inventory accounts are debited, whereas, in perpetual systems, the account's payables are credited. Some organizations also prefer using multi-column purchase journals to record payment transactions. All kinds of purchases involving assets, merchandise, and any other type of holdings are recorded together in the multi-column journal entry. Specific columns can be used to enter certain types of payments according to the needs of the organization.

Trade Discount

A trade discount is an amount that is being exempted from the actual catalog price whenever a sale is made. The discount is offered to the buyer by the supplier or seller. Trade discounts are offered by sellers in order to earn a definite percentage of profit by selling these goods. For example, a trader may be selling a commodity at $100, including a discount of 5% on the selling price. The trader has the option of giving the buyer a benefit for selling the commodity by granting him a discount of 5%. This also means that the buyer will be able to sell the commodity to his customers at $95. The trade discount is not recorded on any of the books by the accountants since these discounts will not change the accounts for either the buyer or the seller. The trade discounts are only shown in the invoice in the form of a small deduction from the actual selling price of the commodity. In the journals that are used for recording purchases and sales, the actual sale value or the net purchase value is recorded after the discount is deducted from the value of the goods that are shown in the books or journals.

Sales Book

The purpose of the sales book is similar to that of the purchase book. In these accounts, only the sales that are made on credit will be recorded. All the additional details of the sale, including the name of the customer and the date of the transaction, will be recorded in this particular section of the journal. The sales books are prepared according to the copies of the invoices that are sent out to the customers. The account of the individual customer will be debited with the amount individually whenever it is posted in the sale spoke at the beginning or end of every month or fiscal period. After this is done, the sales account will then be credited with the total amount that is mentioned in the sales book. All the other sales that have been made through cash will be recorded separately in a different cashbook.

Purchase Returns Book

All details that are associated with financial transactions involving goods or merchandise that is returned by a business or a customer to its supplier will be recorded in the purchase returns the book. It is important to keep in mind that the purchase returns book will only record the returns of credit purchases and not cash purchases. IF a certain purchase is returned, and the purchase was initially made on a cash basis, it will not be recorded into the purchase returns the book. If a commodity or merchandise needs to be returned to a supplier or seller, then a debit note will also be sent to the same supplier along with the product that is being returned. This debit note is sent for the purpose of indicating that the particular account will be debited with the amount that is mentioned within the debit note. The total amount from the purchase return book will be credited to the purchases return account towards the end of every month. Apart from this, even the individual accounts of all the suppliers who have received the debit notes will also be individually debited.

Sales Return Book

In any business practice, there will be certain times when a customer may want to return the goods that they have purchased by them for certain reasons, whatever it may be. It may be due to low-quality concerns or even due to quantity issues. Therefore, the details of all these commodities that have been returned by customers or buyers also need to be kept track of and recorded in the books of accounts of the business. All such entries are maintained in the Sales Return book. All the financial transactions wherein the goods or commodities had been sold for cash will not be recorded in the sales return book; only sales that have been made on credit will be recorded in the sales return book. Whenever a customer returns a product, the business is required to send a credit note to the customer, informing them that his or her account will be credited with the monetary value of the goods that are returned by them. This amount is debited from the sales returns the book to the sales returns account, whereas individual accounts of customers who have returned goods will also be credited with the same amount.

Bills Receivable Book

The bills receivable book is a journal that is used for recording all the financial transactions involving payments that the business has yet to receive from its contractors or customers in the future. All the entries that are recorded in this book will include the date of billing or receipt of the bill, the acceptor's name, and the due date for payment, the total amount payable, the terms of payment and other financial details. The total amount that is obtained from the column of the bills receivable book will be debited to the Bills Receivable Account, and the individual payments that are to be received from other customers will be credited to their respective accounts.

Bills Payable Book

All the information or particulars that are available in the Bills Payable book are accepted by most businesses for the purpose of repaying a specific sum of money or due payments at a future date. All these details are recorded in the Bills Payable book for this very reason. It essentially serves the purpose of showing all the due payments that the business has to make to its creditors. Therefore, the acceptance of the bills payable will be returned to the drawer eventually. The amount of every individual bill will be posted on the debit side of the drawer's account in the ledger, whereas the total amount obtained from the bills payable book will be posted to the credit of the bills payable account in the same nature.

Cashbook

The Cashbook is a record of all financial transactions concerning cash receipts as well as cash payments that your business or firm may be involved in. It is a common thing for the cash flow to be affected by financial transactions on a daily basis. This could happen in the form of cash sales, payment of different overheads or expenses such as wages, salaries, commissions, water bills, electricity bills, property taxes, or rent. Considering this, the need for maintaining different/separate cashbooks or ledgers for recording different types of financial transactions cannot be overemphasized any further. The most important function of a cashbook is to record all the cash receipts or cash payments of the business on a daily basis. All the cash that is received by the business or the money that is flowing into the business is recorded on the debit side of the Cashbook, whereas all cash payments that are made to other parties are recorded on the credit side of the book. Cash transactions of most companies tend to be the largest for any business and require the most amount of bookkeeping to keep it updated on a daily basis. If every financial transaction that is made in cash is recorded in the primary journal books, it will require an unnecessarily large amount of labor and effort for crediting and debiting the cash account every single time any cash is received or paid. It is through the Cashbook that all this unnecessary effort and hassle of including every cash payment or item of receipt individually in the cash account of a ledger can be easily avoided, making the accounting process easier.

Chapter 6: CashFlow, Functions And

Working Capital For Effective

Accounting

In this chapter we are going to look closely on the flow of cash through the business, its role and functions, how it is generated, its source and uses and also the working capital within the firm.

There's been quite a myriad of concerns with modern businesses and how they have manipulated rules of accounting to portray profits that do not really reflect economic reality, although they perceive to have followed the technical guidelines, slightly deviating from the standards set by accounting bodies.

Cash Flow in Detail

In the case of cash, this is free of judgment but is most likely to not give the precise value of a firm's performance.

It is important to know that a business perceives flow of two entities, that is the profit flow and cash flow within the business, and both are derived at differently. Cash flow involves inflow and outflow, doesn't leave room for any creativity while cash moves in and out of a business. Profit flow allows legitimate ways of adjustment to arrive at the true value of profit, cash shows reality by the movement of money, at least this is how it is designed to be perceived.

For any new project introduced by the firm, it needs cash and approval of budget from the finance director who decides if the firm has substantial cash to run the project. A firm doesn't go bankrupt when it incurs losses, but it does when it is running out of cash to settle its debts and liabilities.

Although cash flow does not say much about a firm's performance or its level of success or failure, it is vital as it determines short term viability for the firm to operate. If we are considering a 12 year plan for a firm, unless we see to it that the firm has cash to operate for every of the 12 years. If not it will not work. Managing cash is there key to operating a business. This is rather a continuous process of generating the apt flow of cash rather than holding cash still and saving it for the rainy days. This obviously means that cash needs to be used to purchase equipment for the firm. If cash does not flow and is saved on every little bit of equipment, then machinery could get outdated over time and this can cause problems to the success of the business.

Although bankers perceive to aid entrepreneurs with cash to start a business, in reality they do not give cash without maximum benefit they go into agreement a lender. Going overdraft can cause entrepreneurs to become overly dependent of bank manager's decision to further settle a loan payment. Bank lending usually works on a certain working capital ratio which companies struggle to meet. However, since they like to keep up to loan covenants, they operate under these set ratios. However, this causes decision making power to shift to banks who then monopolize the business.

Why do we need Cash?

The saying that money is not plucked from the trees often rings a bell. Therefore, money is made. Now why is money made? There has to be some purpose on making money! Here it is subdivided into categories below as to what the purpose of money is for a business.

To make a transaction, for example, any usual day to day transaction of a business like paying utility bills

For precautionary measures, to pay off for any unexpected event

For Speculation, when trying to invest on a new business, or purchasing shares of a running business

Now let us look into each purpose more carefully.

Paying Bills: The company needs to have cash to settle bills when they are due as paying on time is an important factor that builds and maintains the reputation of the firm. It can also create a long term good impression to suppliers at times when the business is running low.

Paying Suppliers: Suppliers provide on credit under specific timings for settlement based on government rules or at time privately negotiated between firms and suppliers. Usually payments are agreed to be made at the month end following the month of delivery. The current trend of businesses permitting customers maximum time to pay is causing companies to struggle.

Paying interest accumulated from loans: - Bankers expect payments to be made regularly to settle accumulating interest and part of the

principle loan that they have lent a firm. Taking the right amount of loan is vital for any business to operate. Knowledge of Accounting and cash flow can give an approximate idea of how much the firm is able to repay monthly. Excessive loans can bring down a company to bankruptcy when banks eventually decide to stop lending. This causes further problems where the company suffers to settle the existing loans.

Paying tax: - Governments keep track of businesses and how they make money. The tax authorities will request tax payment in cash when they discover that the profit has reached a certain threshold that is becomes liable to tax.

Working Capital Inflation: - Inflation has an effect on working capital. Let's consider a case where you have 500 items of inventories at the beginning of the year, the cost of each being $1.00 each. If the remaining stock at the end of the year is 500 but the cost has risen to

$1.05 each due to the increase in price of raw material and labor caused by inflation by 5%. This is the extra cost of $25 for stock has to be put into the business in terms of cash that was earned throughout the year.

Optional payments: - For this, companies have a choice to think and decide the right time to purchase and to pay. Few months could be better on cash flow than others.

Companies need to be careful not to commit to dealings below at a time that cash flow is low.

Capital expenditure: - Non-current assets are purchased by cash. There are options to buy in instalments or loans thus creating a cash reserve

to operate the business. Companies usually allocate a budget every year to control capital expenditure and they weigh their choices and invest very carefully as once spent, the payments are quite irreversible. This can have a significant effect on the cash flow. For example, if an employee is hired, he has to be paid. Therefore cash is already committed to. If the company wants to acquire a building, then cash is already spent on local councils.

Suppliers can be paid monthly but when deciding to buy a new property, the decision is optional and depends on management

Acquisition of other Firms: - This is done by offering cash to the other firm or buying shares. They may alternatively offer shares or loan notes in exchange to purchasing shares from a company. However, cash attracts more investors as this gives the real value as opposed to company shares that could only offer perceived value. Although cash offers are usually lower, research shows that acquisition is usually agreed by cash as compared to those issued by shares. In cases where an acquisition is made with exchange of shares, it is usually down with a part payment of cash that helps to finalize the deal. Cash acquisitions are very rare these days owing to the large sum of money that has to be settled that is also taxable by governments.

Paying dividends:- They are often paid to owners and shareholders in cash. Alternatively, some agree to be paid with additional shares. Paying dividends through shares helps to retain cash. Dividends are settled also to maintain confidence in the stock market. If dividends remain constant over time, then this is word of warning. If it gets lower

then this is something that needs immediate action to be taken. If companies fail to settle dividends as they did as a trend for a couple of years, then this will result in shareholders selling out. Therefore dividends are considered to be compulsory payments that have to be settled mandatorily. Failure to do so exposes the company to everyone around as failing and will be losing their image, reputation and credibility.

5.1 Sources of Cash

We have understood, so far, the importance of cash to run a business. Now we are going to see where cash can be obtained from. Cash can be high only when the business is operating well. We already mentioned about the concept of high risks yielding higher returns. Therefore the more the investment and borrowings, the higher is the expected return from shareholders and bankers.

So how is cash put into a business?

1. Shareholders invest directly or indirectly into the business. Setting aside a part of the profit is an effective way to increase cash. This can be done by utilizing the profits that are gained

by cash flows and saving some than to distribute all amounts as dividends to shareholders. Therefore by this retention, shareholders are indirectly investing more into the business. Another option is for shareholders to agree on more shares in the place of cash dividends

Shareholders may choose to buy more shares if the company has created a good reputation for returns in the past.

Either ways, the investment of the business rises thus leading to higher returns and more cash generated.

2.   From Bankers and Lenders:- Here cash is obtained by borrowing in short-term such as overdraft or long-term such as bank loans. Overdrafts are charged high on interest, although bank

loans can be agreed at a lower rate of interest. Long term loans should be settled at the end of the agreed term while overdrafts can be settled anytime the company has money to pay. If banks have agreed for a certain period of loan, then they cannot decide later to demand return earlier. They often agree for loans based on an asset as security.

A viable plan for a firm would be to retain a higher portion of non- current asset than its loan or approximately 1.5 times higher value of current assets than its current liability. This mitigates potential risk of non-payment of bank loans and keeps the business in a safe position.

Other than banks, other large companies issue debts in the form of debentures where investors can buy and sell stock as loans. If it is agreed that loan stocks cannot be redeemed, the yearly interest alone is payable. Here the cost of cash is high and also greater tendency for the company to become insolvent.

3. Effective management of working capital :- The underlying principle here is that the lower the inventories and debtors or the higher the creditors, the more cash within the firm. A vital factor here is the loss of opportunity when inventories are not sold. It just shows the performance of the company to be under- performing. Another factor that plays a part on increasing cash flow is by reducing debtor's payment period. However, again if there's competition offering longer credit periods, customers can easily balk a business and change its suppliers. Suppliers can be requested longer

periods of credit. However, they may agree only if they manage to negotiate a higher price.

4.   Selling a business:- When a company is unable to return the loans, they tend to sell their business, wholly or partly. The hitch here is whether someone will be willing to pay a high price for what they know you want to sell. They are at higher bargaining power and one might be in a position to sell out of compulsion. This is now acquisition takes place. The cost in selling a business is where the business stops generating cash from the part that is meant to be sold. So valuing this loss of cash is the factor that determines the price you could sell the business for.

Forecasting and Managing Cash – Inflow, Outflow and Balance Sheet

Cash of a business could be managed efficiently if a plan is strategized foreseeing the future of the firm's growth. Owners should be able vision the future to identity what they need to do now to gain foresee potential success and mitigate risks that could hinder the way of progress.

Forecasting cash flow is a short term focus that looks at how the business could manage in case of any unforeseen financial difficulties. Although Cash management may be short term, it plays a vital role in handling a situation of crisis in the business.

Cash Flow Management is the most essential part of accounting that determines the success of a business. It is through this information that a bank could approve a loan.

www.ingramcontent.com/pod-product-compliance
Lightning Source LLC
Chambersburg PA
CBHW071707210326
41597CB00017B/2374